Date: 7/31/12

J 513.211 ATW
Atwood, Megan.
Busy beavers : counting by 5s

BUSY BEAVERS: COUNTING BY 5S

by Megan Atwood

illustrated by Sharon Holm

Content Consultant: Paula J. Maida, PhD

magic wagon

VISIT US AT
WWW.ABDOPUBLISHING.COM

Printed in the United States of America, North Mankato, Minnesota.
102011
012012

 THIS BOOK CONTAINS AT LEAST 10% RECYCLED MATERIALS.

Text by Megan Atwood
Illustrations by Sharon Holm
Edited by Lisa Owings
Interior layout and design by Christa Schneider
Cover design by Christa Schneider

Library of Congress Cataloging-in-Publication Data

Atwood, Megan.
  Busy beavers : counting by 5s / by Megan Atwood ; illustrated by Sharon Lane Holm.
      p. cm. — (Count the critters)
  ISBN 978-1-61641-852-6
  1. Counting—Juvenile literature. 2. Set theory—Juvenile literature. I. Holm, Sharon Lane, ill. II. Title.
  QA113.A89 2012
   513.2'11 — dc23
                         2011033074

You can count faster when counting by fives. Count by fives while you watch this beaver family build a dam. Count how many sticks they pile up. To count by fives, add five to the last number you counted.

Beavers paddle and play. Baby beavers are called kits. Three kits paddle with sticks. Mother and Father Beaver carry sticks too. The nocturnal beavers carry their sticks at night. Count the sticks slowly: one, two, three, four, five sticks for the dam.

35   40   45   50   0+5=5

Beavers play and paddle. Three beaver kits roll in the water with sticks. Oily fur keeps beavers dry and warm in water. One beaver carries a bundle of sticks to the dam. Count the sticks quickly by fives: five, ten.

One beaver kit chomps on branches to get sticks. His teeth get sharpened as he chews. He carries a bundle of sticks to the dam. Count the sticks by fives: five, ten, fifteen.

35   40   45   50   10+5=15

Beavers chew and chomp. Beaver kits eat leaves, twigs, and bark. Father Beaver carries a bundle of sticks to the dam. Count the sticks by fives: five, ten, fifteen, twenty.

Beavers splish and splash. Three beaver kits splash each other with their tails. One of them carries a bundle of sticks to the dam.

Count the sticks by fives: five, ten, fifteen, twenty, twenty-five.

Beavers splash and splish. Mother and Father Beaver splash the kits! Mother Beaver carries a bundle of sticks to the dam.

That's five more sticks! Count the sticks by fives: five, ten, fifteen, twenty, twenty-five, thirty.

35   40   45   50   25+5=30

Beavers build and burrow. The dam is almost done! Mother Beaver swims toward the dam with another bundle of sticks. Count the sticks by fives: five, ten, fifteen, twenty, twenty-five, thirty, thirty-five.

31 32 33 34 **35**   40   45   50   30+5=35

Beavers burrow and build. Mother
Beaver burrows into the dam to see
if it is strong. It needs more sticks!
Father Beaver carries a bundle of
sticks to the dam. Count the sticks
by fives: five, ten, fifteen, twenty,
twenty-five, thirty, thirty-five, forty.

35　36 37 38 39 **40**　45　50　35+5=**40**

Beavers build and burrow. The three beaver kits are getting tired. Mother and Father Beaver help them carry another bundle of sticks to the dam.

Count the sticks by fives: five, ten, fifteen, twenty, twenty-five, thirty, thirty-five, forty, forty-five.

35 40 41 42 43 44 **45** 50 40+5=45

Beavers burrow and build. Father Beaver carries the last bundle of sticks to the dam. It's time to return to the lodge to put the beaver kits to bed. Count the sticks by fives: five, ten, fifteen, twenty, twenty-five, thirty, thirty-five, forty, forty-five, fifty. The dam is done!

35   40   45   46 47 48 49 **50**   45+5=50

Words to Know

bundle—a group of things fastened together so they are easier to handle.

burrow—to dig a shelter underground.

chomp—to bite down hard.

dam—a wall to stop the flow of water.

lodge—a beaver home.

nocturnal—sleeps during the day and is active at night.

Web Sites

To learn more about counting by 5s, visit ABDO Group online at **www.abdopublishing.com**. Web sites about counting are featured on our Book Links page. These links are routinely monitored and updated to provide the most current information available.

5 10 15 20 25 30 35 40 45 50